The sink was blocked. Now it is fixed and the water runs away making a glugging, gurgling sound, *g, g, g, g*.

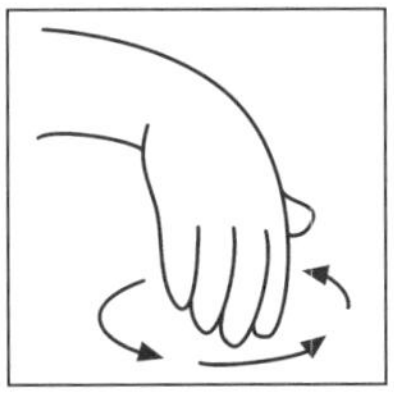

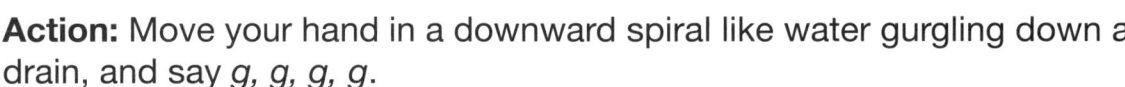

Action: Move your hand in a downward spiral like water gurgling down a drain, and say *g, g, g, g*.

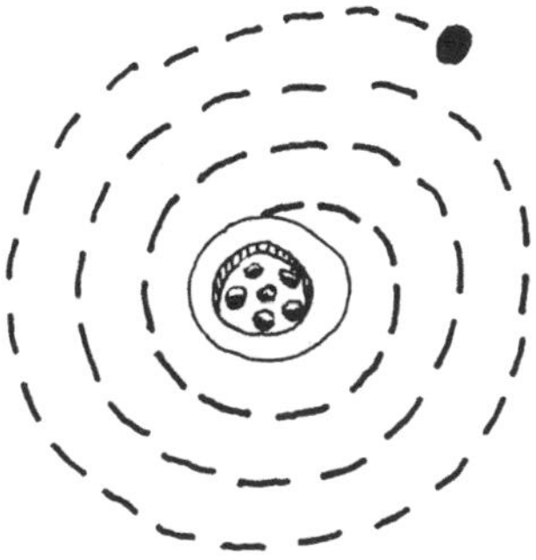

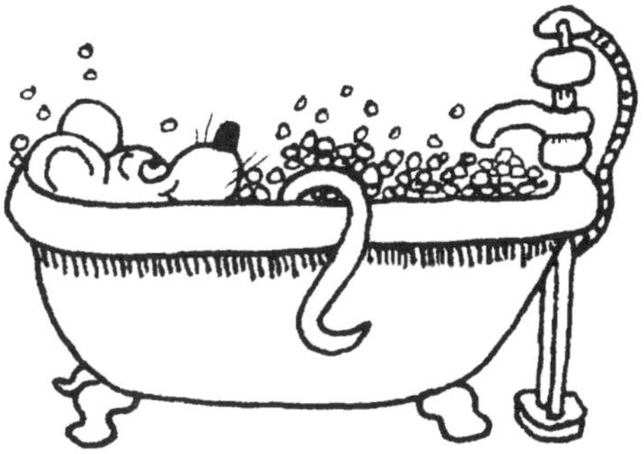

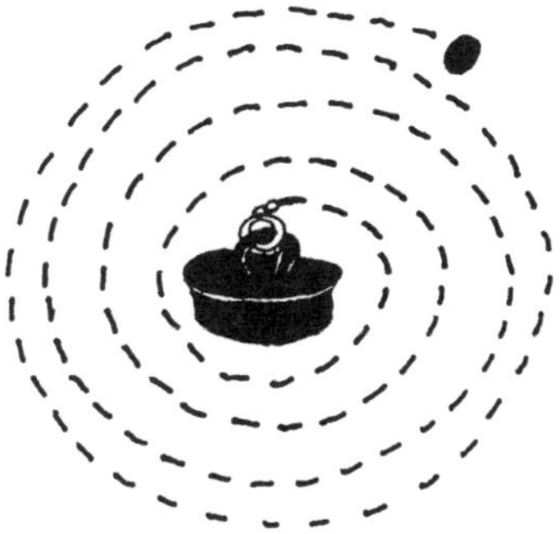

g

g g g g g g

g g g g g g

Write in the missing letter, starting from the dot.

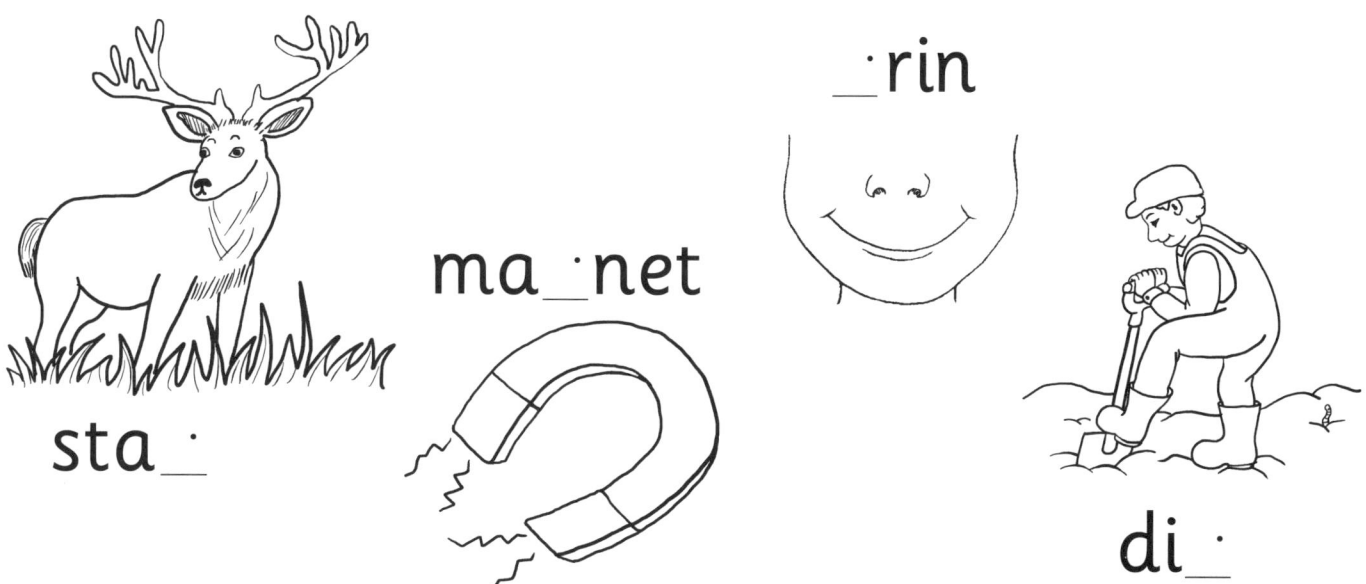

sta_

ma_net

_rin

di_

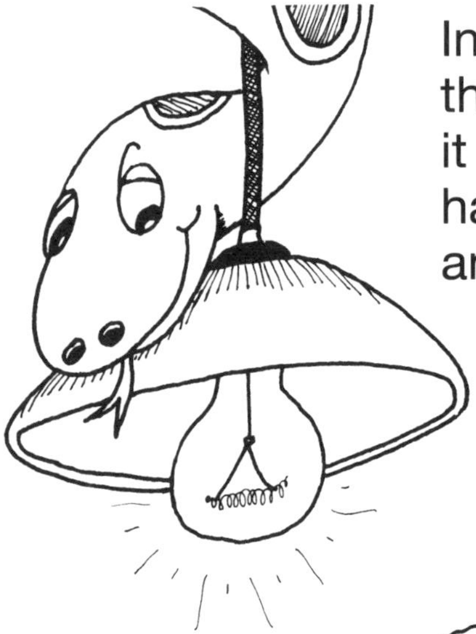

Inky finds a switch near the bookshelf. She presses it a few times to see what happens. The light goes on and off, *o-o, o-o*.

O o

Action: Pretend to turn a light switch on and off, and say *o-o, o-o*.

o

s_ck

r_ck

h_p

d_g

Bee has a new umbrella. She puts it up in the rain – *u, u, u, up, umbrella!*

U u

Action: Keep one hand steady and raise the other as if putting up an umbrella, and say *u, u, u, u*.

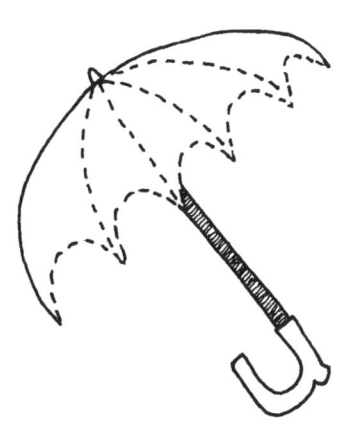
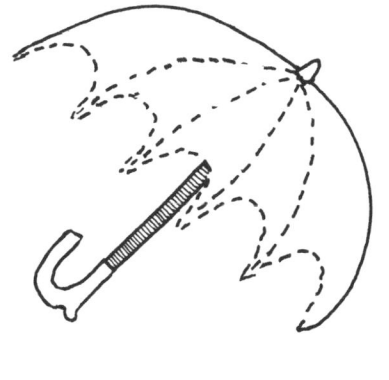

up up up
up up up

u

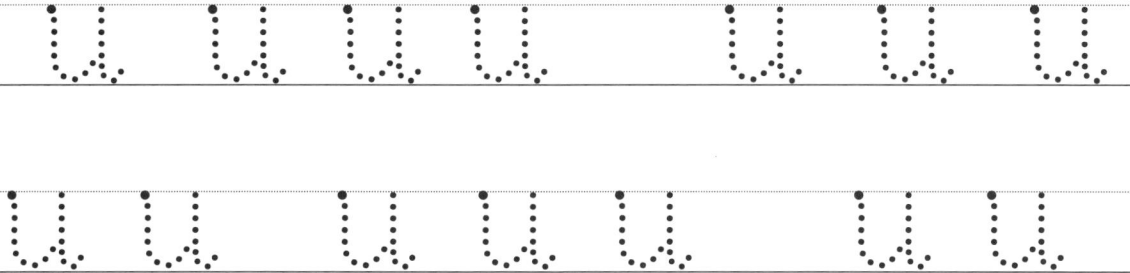

r_g   dr_m   s_n   _p

L l

Snake is licking a lovely lemon lollipop, *lllll*.

Action: Pretend to lick a lollipop, saying *lllll*.

lick a lollipop

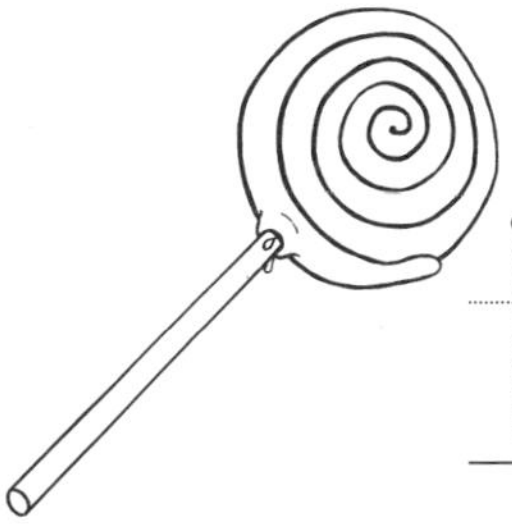

lick a lollipop

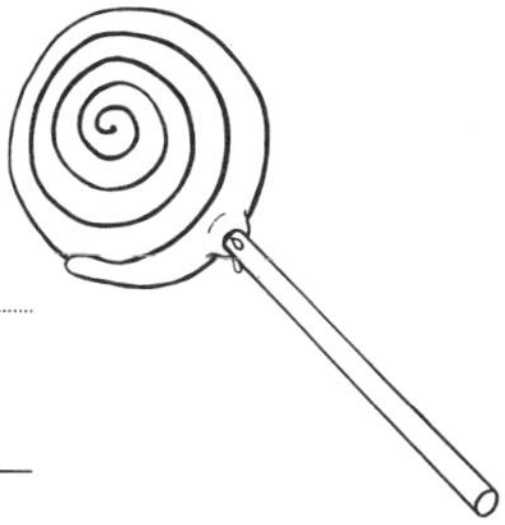

l l l   l   l l l   l l
l l l   l   l l l   l

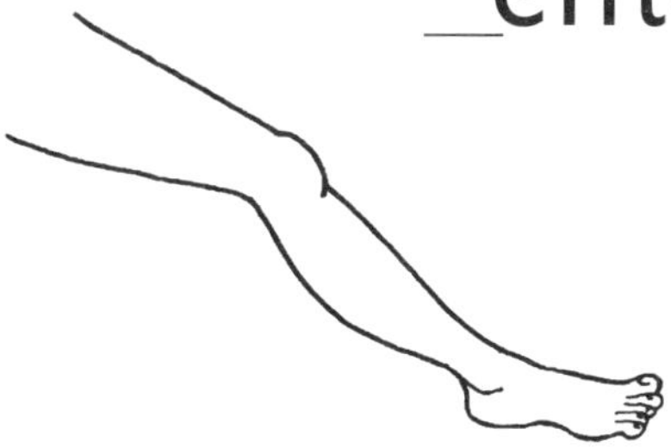

_eg 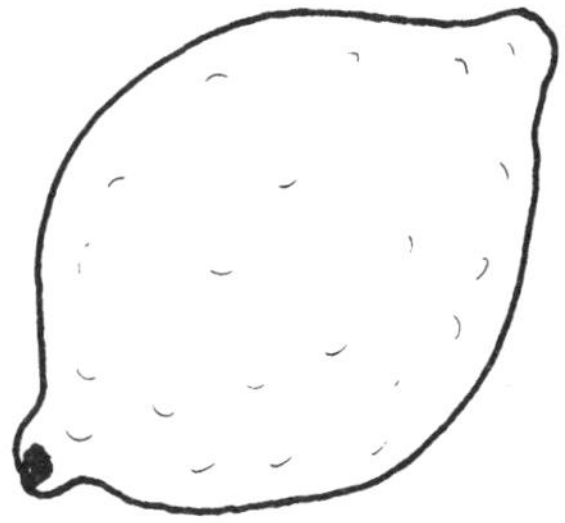
_emon
_og  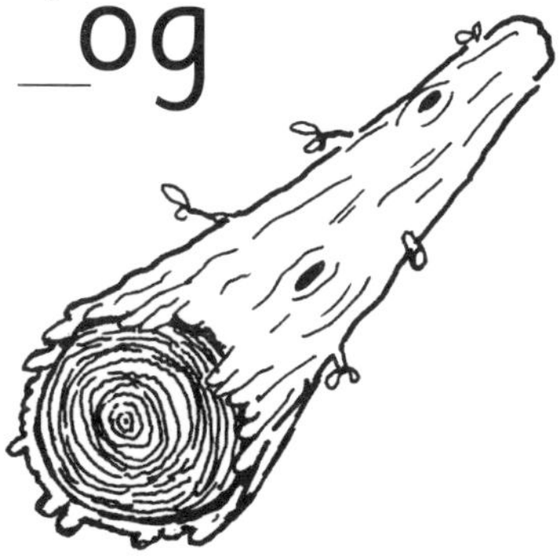
hi_

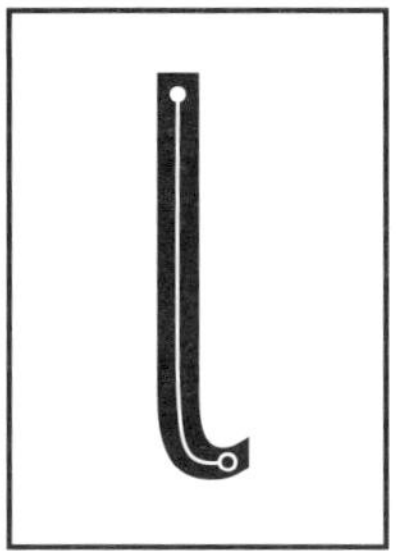

Ff

Snake tries to catch an inflatable fish as it floats by. There is a strange *ffffff* sound and the fish goes flat. Snake's sharp fangs have punctured the fish!

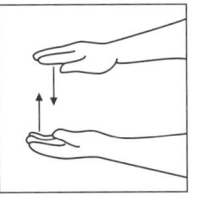

Action: Slowly bring your hands together to mime an inflatable fish deflating, and say *ffffff*.

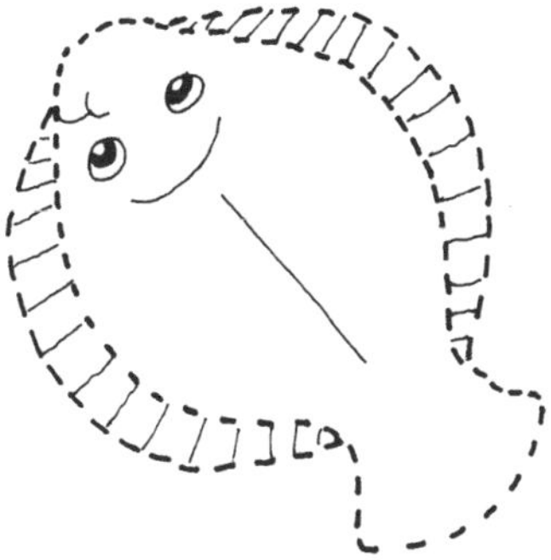

ffffff flat

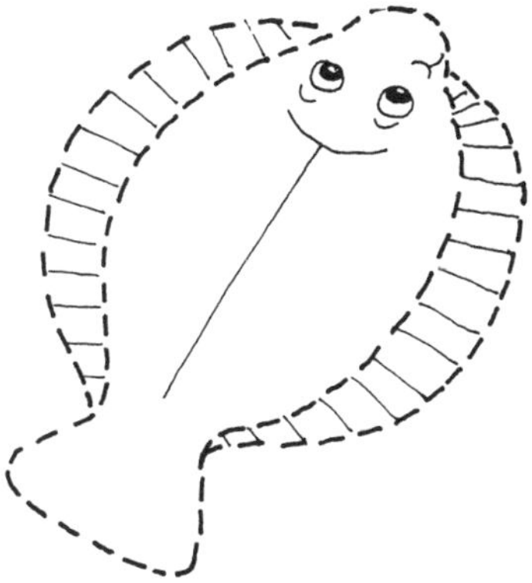

ffffff flat

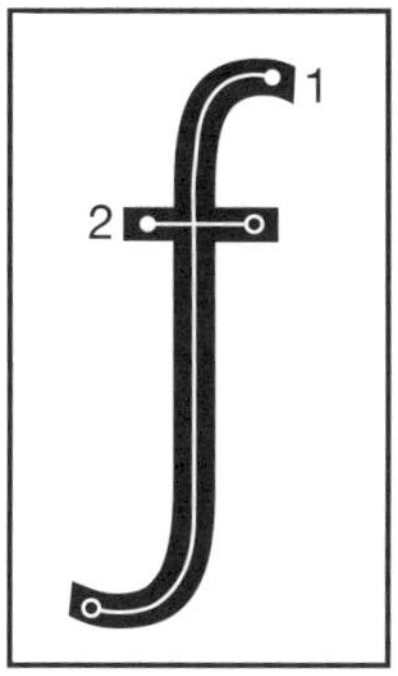

f f f f f f f

f f f f f f

_lag

gi_t

_rog

o__

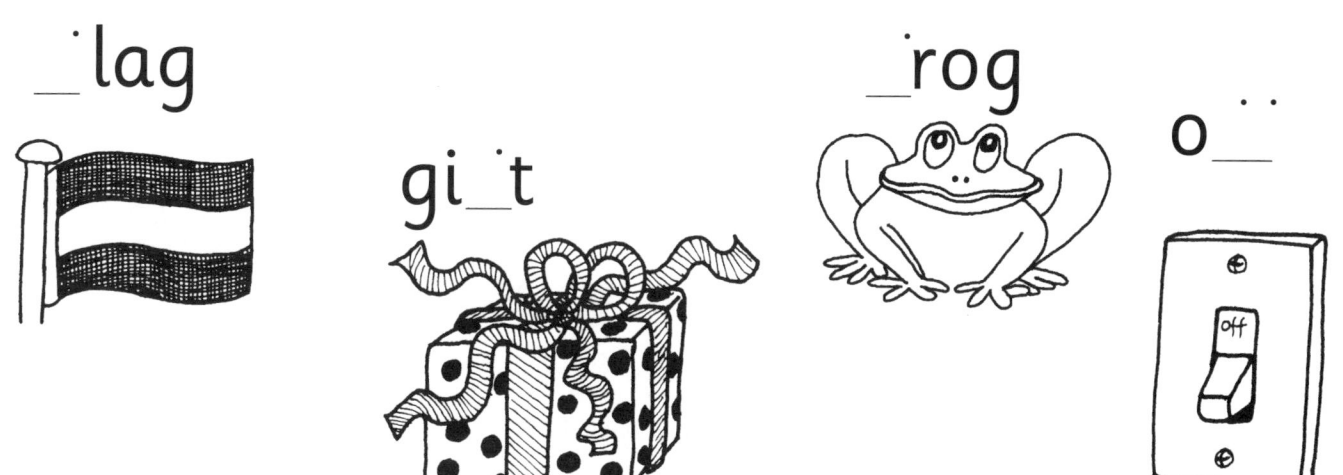

Inky, Snake and Bee are playing in the park. They hit the ball with a bat, *b, b, b, b*.

B b

Action: Pretend to hit a ball with a bat, saying *b, b, b, b*.

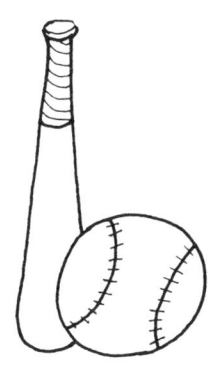

b b b bat

b b b bat

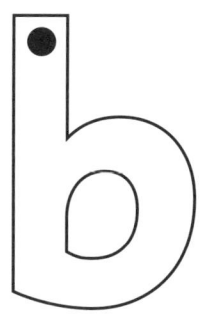

When writing /b/, remember to go down for the bat first, then back up and around for the ball.

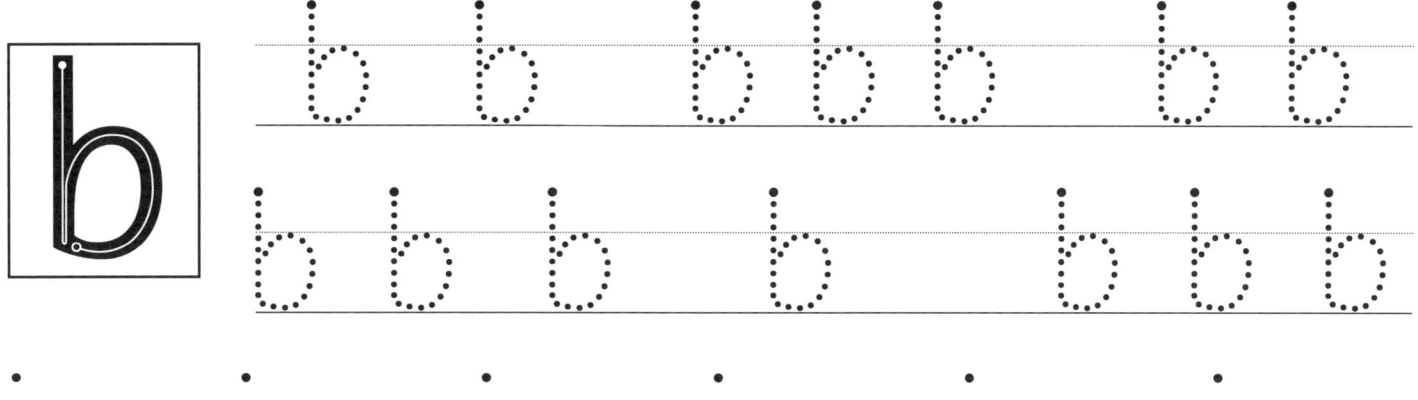

_ell   _elt   ra_ _it   cra_

Say the word for each picture. Does it have the sound in it?

Say the words, listen for the sounds and write the letters on the lines.

u
g
m

a
t
h

t
n
e

n
u
s

d
g
o

t
a
n

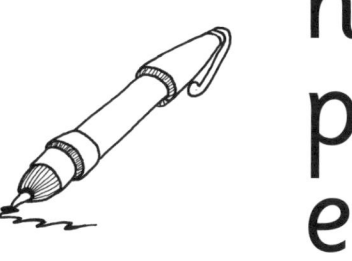
n
p
e

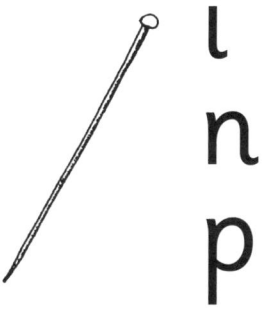
i
n
p

o
t
p

Do you know these sounds? Trace over the dotted letters, then draw a picture of something that begins with each sound.

a	h	l
t	r	u
s	c k	f
n	d	o
i	e	b
p	m	g

How quickly can you say the sounds?

Write the letter for the missing sound in each word.

Read the words in the logs. Match each word to the picture in the frog that rhymes with it.

- fun
- red
- mat
- leg
- grab
- log

When two letters that make the same sound come together, you only say the sound once: /r-a-bb-i-t/.

Read each word and draw a picture of it in the space.

rabbit

kitten

dress

hill

duck

parrot

Read the words, choose the right word for each picture and write it underneath.

met mat man   log dig dog   cup cut cap

mat

peg egg big   net nut not   and ant act

hen hat pen   bin bus bug   sob sit sun

Trace over the letters. Then read the word and draw a picture in the space.

hat	pen	ant
ink	man	cap
bed	dog	bus

1   2   3

Count the caterpillars.

  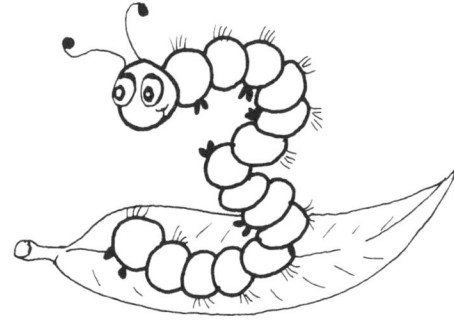

Trace over the dotted lines to write the number 3.

Find the 3 caterpillars.

Activity

Flat fish race

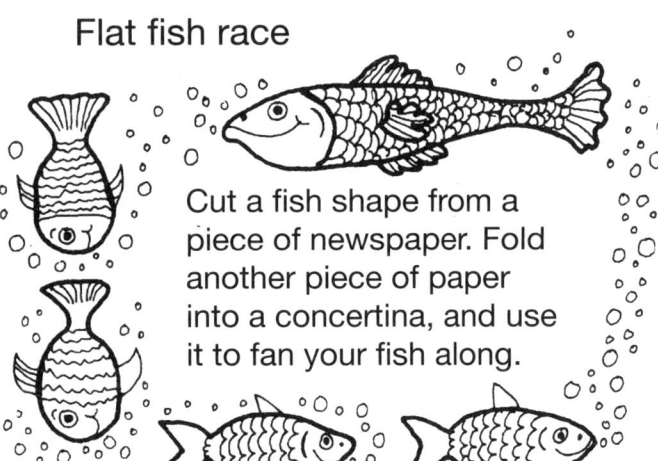

Cut a fish shape from a piece of newspaper. Fold another piece of paper into a concertina, and use it to fan your fish along.

Make a mobile

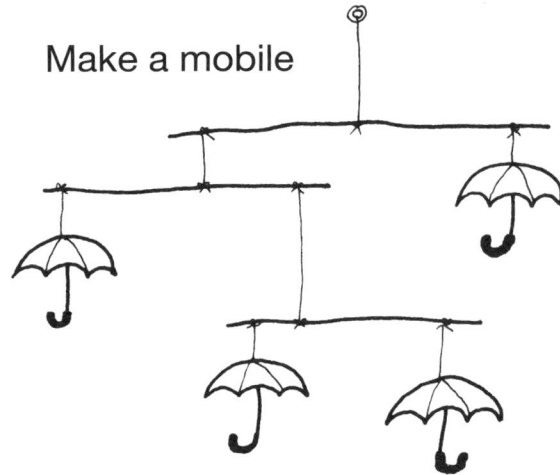

Cut some umbrella shapes from card. Decorate them and hang them as a mobile.

Lemon ice cubes

Make some lemon ice cubes from a lemon drink poured into an ice-cube mould.

Read a story

Read the story of *The Three Billy Goats Gruff*.